UNDRESSED

KHYATI GUPTA

ISBN 979-888530090-2

The book is dedicated to all the dear and near ones I come across daily and specially dedicated to all the rebels out there. The thoughts which I have penned down are a result of the meetings and experincing the things with people who have struggled and made their own life. I am greatfully thankful to my family and my mentors who encouraged me at my worse and stood by me .

Contents

Foreword

This book is basically about a collection of thoughts turned into musings by the author describing the beauty of nature and mind, and threading thoughts together to put them in words which the readers can enjoy. This book doesn't have any educational related content it is basically written to entertain and amuse readers just like the title of the book suggests Amusing Musings.

The author of the book has created a variety of poetries and verses and penned them down for the readers to spend their time reading the poetries and take pleasure in reading.

The author has excellently made the collection where some verses also put your mind to thought that how and where the author relates real life scenes with the verses written.

Enjoy your journey with this book.

Chapter 1

BIRD WITHOUT WINGS
Wings! magical, isn't it?
Ever wondered what it is supposed to mean to a bird
More like a support to break open the grid
The grid that disorients
The grid that is impotent
And a creature like bird
Has to disperse
In the infinite
To strengthen its grip
And let the wings fly
And let the wings explore
How far they can go
How much they can grow
And yet the predators try to take them down
Not appropriate, yes!
But not something which is frowned
This is how it works
The poison always lurks
You have to fight o 'dear bird
Prove it from your flight.

• *Khyati Gupta*

GREY

There you go, accomplished
Fulfilled, did what you wanted to
Now it's my turn
to take charge in the run
No one gives you a magic wand
Even if you get you got to understand
How to go
with the flow
seems like I found mine
magic with a hint of prime
and now I know the way
into the woods not an astray.
Looks like here I am meant to be
To be with my perfect grey
I mixed the colors of my pray
Black white and a pinch of gay
I found my perfect grey
The grey which glorifies my day anyday.

• *KHYATI GUPTA*

MORNINGS FOREVER

The mornings are beautiful
Make you rise and shine

Birds chirping leaves rustling
Flowers turning up to incline
To brighter side of their shrine
Looking at the glory of all that it could bring
Oh! Its past nine
And the needle of the clock in your head
Strikes
this is where you belong
this what you have forgone
amidst the serenity
to the eternity
to stay blissful invariably
for ever and ever and ever...
Khyati Gupta
The earthen pot
Made of mud
What worth does it have
Petty is what it feels
Amongst the copper, brass
Oh! but ashes it carries
For you know
mud is to give life
and in mud all shoves.
The Earthen pot is one to bear it all
for the potential it has
to take in the fall
of something so great

getting so small
that a mere Earthen pot
is chosen to engross.
Khyati Gupta.

A TRAVELLER

They say its not possible to travel through time
Well, let me tell you she does it all the time
A traveler need not a possibility to occur
If she want to travel she will do it without defer.
It just takes some loops in the black hole of her roof
And there she is wandering all alone
Wondering what it is supposed to be
Her memories in a dome?
Or is it just the way she tries to replace
things that caused her pain with somethings to embrace.
Khyati gupta

THE DEVILS KISS

All about a time
A mystery to unwind
An angel of her own kind
Was to befall a crime
Far from the truth she lived
In her own shrine
The powers of mind
Stayed in her confined
A sweet little potato pie
Was the girl defined

Oh wait ! Far away
There was an evil eye
The world knew him as
The devil in his prime
Who desired the girl
But to destroy
They built a wall
They kept her quiet
The angel didn't know
Who, when was right?
She thought it is a game
The gods are drawing her life.
So sweet she was but misery lied
In every move she took to fight .
Little did she know the only road
Was to win the devils core
Deal with him all alone
Make him change his ways of roar.
The perceptions of him took a twirl
When they both had their first word
The lass was a girl to change the world
In the exact way the devil wants
The devil had to break the wall
And fill her heart with crazy love
The angel fell for the trick
Her love for him stronger than brick
At last, all she craved was

The poison lurking devils kiss
By khyati gupta.

A MYSTRY UNDONE

Inside you want to hide
Desire to be her attire
Admire the lass, admire
Find the one to decipher
the instincts conspire
Far away from the world, she severs
Constrained in her mind, so never
Comes near to you, whatsoever
She wants to feel the endeavor
And set her free forever
A marvel she is with a fever
Forgetting the aim, she has to cleaver
The universe is with her
And is going to lead her
To end the misery, she suffers.
And save her world for the better.
Khyati gupta .

LOVE UNRAVELLED

We break each other to an extent that makes us feel like hell
we make each other to an extent it feels like we never left the
heaven
We stay with each other to make sure we feel we both are unique
We leave each other and begone as the other never exists.
The many in me loves many in you

It's not possible to stay a muse.
The love lurks and poison burns
Feels like tables have turned
We going to kiss
We going to hold
My beauty is what you behold
There is going to be an apocalypse
When my lips kiss your lips.
KHYATI GUPTA.
7. A SUFFERED MISERY
I couldn't care less
I don't want you anymore
You caused a mess
Left me lone on the shore.
As I started to fall
you put me behind the bars
of the fears I already had
and left me a broken lass
I couldn't care less
Don't want you anymore
The closer I got
The poorer I felt
For choosing you over
And over like hell
I couldn't care less
Don't want you anymore
You standing tall

Is all I recall
Rolled me like a ball
Made me feel like a troll.
I couldn't care less
don't want you anymore
your tricks don't impress
and I couldn't care less
to want you in my life
causing a distress
so here I resign
and let you win the chess
cause I couldn't care less
yes I couldn't care less.
By Khyati gupta

SO, WHAT

I want to succeed while enjoying the way
So, what I want to laugh and play
So, what I never want the child in me hide away
So, what? I still believe in fairy tales.
So, what? A woman in me disappears.
So, what? I react to disrespect.
So, what? I desire a full-fledged love.
So, what? So what?
So, what? A flower doesn't have a single purpose.
The same flower blooms
The fragrance, the beauty, the ambience changes
So what? I offered rose to god instead.

So what? My memory fades.
So what? I create a chaos and am enraged.
So what? I live my life my way.
Khyati Gupta.

THE GIRL KEITH

Your hair like a wreath
That look! Stops my breath
Oh! It gets me high on meth
To describe you
Never have i known
It was hidden beneath
The desire to be your sheath
Want to unleash your heath
And peek in underneath
And just want to be drinking on a reef
Show you all my dreams
Despite of flaws i wanna reach
Reach out to you and then sleeth
Carrying your echo as my bequeath
I sleeth

KHYATI GUPTA

THE NIGHTBLOOD

It cuts deep
The knife of your deeds
Being all hasty to make us feel drasty
It doesn't glorify you
You creature with no noble rules

The wounds you cause
We sew them off
Try to regain the strength that i have lost
But somewhere again
You rip my band aid off
The scars have become a tapestry now
Cannot be seen
But have imprints
Yes! You made a deep cut
But now we have turned a rut
For we have become a nightblood
The deeper you cut
We feel it in our gut
But doesn't matter
Cause now we are nightbloods
Your efforts to seize me can succeed
But you cant stop the breeze
And the breeze i reign
Will set me free
Even in the bars of mighty spree
To hunt down the nigjtbloods like me
But No You wont succeed
KHYATI GUPTA

BURN

Living my life my way
Far from astray yet not a decay
Pulling off things anyway

Zealous and merry
Frolic and gay
Burnt , are you?
Your sky is blue while mine is pink
Yet rising up from dead everyday
Not falling for your tricks and walking away
Always honest and integrate
You dream of a better life
While I , of better intentions
And a world with a place
For everyone with their own pace
No rat race
Just personalities full of grace
Though we are not in the same place
Burnt, are you?
KHYATI GUPTA
VULNERABLE
Strong but vulnerable I stay
To be acknowledged are the words I say
Its deeper than an ocean what I want to convey
Conflicting perceptions having a ballet
Frantic, lunatic as it is displayed
Keeps me on the toes and vulnerable I stay
Yet discretely strong it is portrayed
The moments I live get me swayed back in time
Not holding grudges but ready to slay
If you take me down you can

Because vulnerable I am
But beware to get slammed
Cause I comeback with a bang
If you don't understand in your head you remand.
KHYATI GUPTA
WHISKEY IN A TEACUP
Baffled you as you discovered
The wilderness beneath
Perception of yours sober of me
Can't see the storm rising inside
Cause calm is my face as a mime
The eyes speak as fire burns
Sensitive not hollow it is
The thoughts I keep
Deep and deep
To discover me you got to track the reaps
Always travel the untaken
Like whiskey in a teacup
I am a brazen
KHYATI GUPTA
MOMENT OF WEAKNESS
I took a step
Ahead,
In the moment
I regret
I washed down the memories
I had

Of you and me hitting off, well.
Dancing around
On our favorite song
Like someone has casted a spell
All over us, to dwell
In our own little den
Of love with a bell
Clinging on to tell
Rebel
to stay together
Oh! but I regret
The moment I took a step
Ahead.

KHYATI GUPTA

UNPROCESSED THOUGHTS

I did things I dint wanted to
Just to prove i am one of you
To the rebels out there
You are meant to be wooed
By the life itself and koyel's cooh
Just like you i did things too
To prove the worth
To build a girth
Stay firm and unearth
Yet breathing the dearth
Of acceptance of
something set forth.

Just like you I did things too
To set me free, to let me undo
The conventional ways filled in my hood
And find the me and a hidden buzzing bee
Ringing like alarm to set fire on the tree
The tree that only grew
Hopelessness and fruits, few.
Yes, I did things too.
KHYATI GUPTA
The farm knights.
In the village away from the town.
They live like a clown
Is it?
Houses of mud
No doors to shut
Lot of struggles
is the way they battle
the course of life
yet not recognized
So far
In the village away from the town
They live like a clown
Is it?
Tilling the farms
With their rough arms
Spend days, with no warmth.
In the village away from the town

Work rigorously without frowning upon
Little they get
But no one regrets
Berating their worth
So forth I request
To value the amount
Of efforts tireless
In the village away from the town
They live like a clown, is it?

KHYATI GUPTA

THE KNIGHT BRIDE

Vision so sharp
Eyes so fierce
Admiring is that face
Covered in a veil
White is what she wears
Marching the field of flare
Yet unaware of the battles to bear
She walks with grace
And stands with pride
As a knight she is
Dressed up like a bride.

KHYATI GUPTA

UNDRESSED

Told you to stop
Put your mind at rest
As walking the top

Of thoughts unprocessed
Undressed is what you feel
To talk on little things
Which daily we foresee
Yet decide to stay sealed.
What's left beyond
Is a grave of the song
A bird wanted to sing
For which men waited too long.
Stayed unrest
Struggling the quest
What if you revealed?
Will they make you feel undressed?
KHYATI GUPTA